AMANDA WHITTINGTON

Amanda Whittington was born in Nottingham in 1968. After leaving school, she worked as a freelance journalist for a variety of publications and was a columnist for the *Nottingham Evening Post*.

Her stage plays include *Be My Baby* (Soho Theatre), *Satin 'n' Steel* (Nottingham Playhouse/Bolton Octagon), *Ladies' Day* (Hull Truck), *Bollywood Jane* (Leicester Haymarket), *The Wills's Girls* (Tobacco Factory Bristol/BBC Radio Four), *Players Angels*, *Last Stop Louisa's* and *The Boy on the Hill* (New Perspectives). She has also written three youth theatre plays and a stage adaptation of *Saturday Night and Sunday Morning*.

For more information visit www.amandawhittington.com

Other titles in this series

Amanda Whittington

LADIES
DOWN UNDER

NICK HERN BOOKS

London

www.nickhernbooks.co.uk

A Nick Hern Book

Ladies Down Under first published in Great Britain
as a paperback original in 2007 by Nick Hern Books Limited,
14 Larden Road, London W3 7ST

Cover image courtesy of Hull Truck Theatre Company;
design by Ned Hoste/2h

Typeset by Country Setting, Kingsdown, Kent CT14 8ES
Printed and bound in Great Britain by Biddles, King's Lynn

A CIP catalogue record for this book is available from
the British Library

ISBN 978 1 85459 995 7

Ladies Down Under was first presented by Hull Truck Theatre Company at Hull Truck Theatre on 12 April 2007 with the following cast:

PEARL	Annie Sawle
JAN	Sue McCormick
SHELLEY	Jemma Walker
LINDA	Lucy Beaumont
JOE / BILL / CHARLIE / KOALA BARE	Martin Barrass
TOM / BEN / SHANE DANNY / BONDI BITCH	Damien Warren-Smith

Director   Gareth Tudor Price
Designer   Richard Foxton

LADIES DOWN UNDER

Characters

PEARL, *a retired fish-packer, mid-fifties*

JAN, *her workmate, mid-forties*

SHELLEY, *her workmate, mid-twenties*

LINDA, *her workmate, mid-twenties*

TOM, *a volunteer firefighter*

JOE, *Jan's boyfriend*

BILL, *a flight attendant*

BEN, *a flight attendant*

SHANE, *a surfer*

CHARLIE, *an aristocratic dropout*

DANNY, *a traveller*

KOALA BARE, *a drag queen*

BONDI BITCH, *a drag queen*

All male parts can be played by two actors.

The play is set in Manchester and various locations in Australia, February–March 2007.

ACT ONE

Scene One

February 2007. Australia. Blue Mountains. Night.

A bushfire is blazing out of control. Enter JOE, *with a backpack, facing the fire.*

JOE. No! No way!

> *Enter* TOM, *a volunteer firefighter.*

TOM. Hey? Where do you think you're going?

JOE. How do I get out of here?

TOM. You don't. Not till it's under control.

JOE. But I've got to get to Sydney.

TOM. You'll be six feet under if you don't back off.

JOE. There must be a way around it?

TOM. Mate, the roads are closed, the power's down, there's bushfires right across the mountains.

JOE. I'm stuck here?

TOM. Don't panic. Get back to Lithgow, you'll be safe there.

JOE. But I'm meeting Jan, my girlfriend, she's flying in tomorrow.

TOM. Mate, I'm not asking you. Move it!

JOE. No!

> TOM *tries to push* JOE *away, but he pulls free and looks desperately into the fire.*

No . . .

> JOE *throws down his backpack in despair.*

Scene Two

Same time. Manchester Airport. Departures.

Enter PEARL, *with tickets in hand. She looks up at the departure board, then beyond it. She wears a T-shirt with* GIRLS ON TOUR *and her name printed on the front. On the back, football-style, is printed* AUSTRALIA *and a big* 07.

Enter JAN, *in a* GIRLS ON TOUR *T-shirt, with a Boots' carrier bag.*

JAN. Pearl, I found 'em.

Beat.

Pearl?

PEARL. What?

JAN takes a packet of tights from the bag.

JAN. Tights. And they could save your life.

PEARL. Compression stockings? No, ta.

JAN. Do you want to go down with DVD? It's one-in-ten on long-haul flights.

PEARL. DVT.

JAN. We're a high-risk group, you and me, at our age.

PEARL. I'll drink lots of water and wiggle me toes.

JAN. But if your leg swells or if there's any sign of tenderness –

PEARL. It won't.

JAN. I've already put mine on in the ladies.

Beat.

I had to go again. The Imodium's not touched it.

PEARL. You need to eat a bit of something. Settle your stomach.

JAN. I couldn't.

PEARL. Jan, you're only flying. Thousands do it every day. All you've got to do is sit back and let it happen.

JAN. For twenty-four hours.

PEARL. Thirty-six. We stop off in Singapore.

JAN. You mean Dubai?

PEARL. Dubai an' all, but you'll be all right, they've got shops.

JAN. You never said we stopped twice.

PEARL. Well, I didn't know myself till the tickets came.

JAN. Dubai I can just about handle. Singapore . . .

PEARL. It'll be an interesting cultural experience.

JAN. I dread to think what the loos are like.

PEARL. Jan, relax.

JAN. How can I, with my IBS as it is?

PEARL. You've not got IBS. You're just a bit keyed up, that's all. You'll be fine once you board.

JAN. Caught short in a confined space, it's my worst nightmare.

PEARL. You'll have food and drinks and telly, you'll be fine.

JAN. That's easy for you to say, you're a seasoned traveller.

PEARL. I've been to Majorca once.

JAN. Well, that's one more than me. I mean, what am I doing? I'm forty-five years old. I've never been nowhere, I've never done nothing and suddenly here I am, going all the way down under –

PEARL. Jan, is this about Joe?

JAN. No.

PEARL. Is it?

Beat.

JAN. He's been gone all this time. He's travelled all over, he's met interesting people.

PEARL. You're interesting.

JAN. How? Name one thing that's interesting about me?

PEARL. Well . . .

JAN. See.

PEARL. You're just yourself, Jan, and that's what he wants.

JAN. But I'm hardly a beach babe.

PEARL. He didn't go for that.

JAN. But he's been there on Bondi with all them leggy blondes –

PEARL. Still wrote to you, didn't he? Still phoned every week?

JAN. Yeah, but –

PEARL. Still rang you this weekend and said he'd see you in Arrivals?

Beat.

JAN. I know.

PEARL. So what's your problem?

JAN. Nine months, we'd been together. Thirty-six weeks. Nine months together and eleven months apart.

PEARL. But you've known him for years. Joe's a man of his word. If he says he'll be waiting, he'll be there.

TANNOY (*voice-over*). Please be advised that smoking is not permitted in the terminal building, except in designated areas.

JAN. Airports. Boyfriends. Being wanted. Them kind of things don't happen to me.

PEARL. Nor does winning half a million on the horses, but you did.

JAN. We did.

PEARL. Been a hell of a ride, hasn't it?

JAN. I'll say.

PEARL. Your Claire going off to uni.

JAN. In a brand new car all bought and paid for.

PEARL. Both our mortgages gone.

JAN. You retired.

PEARL. Having breakfast every morning in my nice new conservatory, thinking of you off to the fish plant.

JAN. Seems like a long time since we were all there today.

Enter SHELLEY *and* LINDA, *laden with duty-free bags and both wearing* GIRLS ON TOUR *T-shirts.*

SHELLEY. Linda, they're here.

PEARL. Eh up, here comes trouble.

JAN. Spot the spendaholic, eh?

SHELLEY *is showing off her digital camera.*

LINDA. Show 'em what you got, Shell.

SHELLEY. It's called a Canon IXUS 750 7.1 MP, 3 x optical zoom. Fits lovely in your handbag.

LINDA. How much was it?

SHELLEY. How do I know? I said to him in Comet, 'I don't want the cheap 'uns you sell to the chavs.' I could tell he was impressed.

LINDA *has a camera of her own.*

LINDA. I got this.

SHELLEY. Disposable? Linda, it's digital or nowt these days.

LINDA. Seven ninety-nine with free developing.

SHELLEY. You're a woman of substance now. You can't shop in Superdrug.

LINDA. I like Superdrug. They had these on BOGOF, I got us one each.

SHELLEY. Well, go on then.

LINDA. What?

SHELLEY. Take me.

LINDA. Take you where?

PEARL. She wants a photo.

SHELLEY *poses for the camera.*

LINDA. Smile, then.

PEARL. Show us them new teeth you've got.

JAN. Fangs.

SHELLEY. Veneers, thank you.

LINDA *takes a picture.*

LINDA. Lovely.

JAN. Well, you can tell Jerry Hall her job's safe.

LINDA. Jan? Pearl?

JAN *and* PEARL *pose for a photograph.*

SHELLEY. Tell Laurel and Hardy.

LINDA. That were a nice one.

PEARL. Right; now we're finally all here, can we go for a *latte*?

SHELLEY. Or a bottle of champagne?

PEARL. Not yet. Jan needs to eat.

LINDA. They've got some lovely-looking muffins in Costa.

PEARL. Could you stomach that, Jan?

LINDA. Chocolate chip?

JAN. I could give it a go.

LINDA. I'll get you one. I'll get us all one.

JAN. You've already bought us drinks on the train.

LINDA. I don't mind. I want to.

PEARL. You spend too much on us.

SHELLEY. She can afford it. She's still working full-time.

JAN. Unlike you, who's done bugger all from the day of the win.

SHELLEY. I'm getting into modelling. I've been working on my look.

PEARL. For all this time?

JAN. And perhaps you should look at your bank balance occasionally?

SHELLEY. I do. I'm in the black for the first time in years and what I do with all them noughts is my business.

LINDA. Shall we not talk about the money?

JAN. I'm just saying –

LINDA. I know, but shall we not? We're meant to be getting away from it all.

SHELLEY. We wouldn't be going without it.

LINDA. But we don't have to go on about it, do we? All the time. On and on and –

TANNOY (*voice-over*). Will passengers for Flight BASD35Z to Sydney, please proceed to Gate 12.

PEARL. Sydney? Bloody hell, that's us.

JAN. Already?

SHELLEY. You lose track with all them shops.

JAN. Is this it?

PEARL. Not quite. There'll be a bit more queuing first.

LINDA. I just want to get on with it.

SHELLEY. I want a drink.

JAN. I want to go home.

SHELLEY. Oh no you don't.

JAN. I can't do it. I can't fly all that way. What if summat goes wrong?

SHELLEY. Then we tragically die.

LINDA. And at least we'd be together.

PEARL. But it won't.

JAN. Concorde crashed.

PEARL. And how many millions haven't?

SHELLEY. You know what fear of flying really is? Fear of sex. I read an article.

JAN. Oh, and what's fear of bombs? Fear of being blown to bits, perchance?

PEARL. Jan, you're not going to die, all right? None of us are. At least, not in the next four weeks, I swear.

LINDA. Just think of the sunshine.

PEARL. Think of us.

SHELLEY. Think of what a prat you'd look at work if you go home.

JAN. I know. It's just a big thing, that's all.

LINDA. It is for me.

SHELLEY. And I've only ever been to Fuengirola.

PEARL. So you break it down. Take it moment by moment. Do a bit, then a bit more, then a bit more than that.

TANNOY (*voice-over*). Will passengers for Flight BASD35Z to Sydney, please proceed to Gate 12.

JAN. Australia. Us?

LINDA. Lovely beaches.

SHELLEY. Lovely men.

PEARL. Uluru.

SHELLEY. Eh?

PEARL. Ayer's Rock, we've got to see that.

JAN. I can't imagine . . .

PEARL. You don't have to. You can see it all for yourself.

LINDA. And you won't be on your own.

SHELLEY. You've got money in your pocket.

PEARL. You've got Joe.

Beat.

JAN. It is a dream come true, I suppose.

SHELLEY. It's what other people do every day. Why not us?

LINDA. The journey of a thousand miles begins with one step.

PEARL. So best foot forward, eh?

LINDA. For Joe?

Beat.

JAN. For Joe.

Exit JAN, followed by SHELLEY and LINDA.

PEARL. Best foot forward.

Exit PEARL.

Scene Three

An hour later. Aeroplane. The engines are revving up. The women are in their seats, PEARL and JAN on one side of the aisle, LINDA and SHELLEY on the other.

Two male flight attendants (BILL and BEN) demonstrate the emergency procedure.

BILL. Good evening and welcome aboard British Airways

Flight BASD35Z from Manchester. If you're going to
Sydney, you're in the right place.

BEN. If you're not, you're in for a long night.

BILL. My name's Bill.

BEN. And my name's Ben.

BILL. And we're here to talk you through the emergency
procedure.

JAN. Is your mobile off? They interfere with the electrics.

PEARL. I've left it at home.

JAN. Mine won't work out there, I checked.

BILL. British Airways are pleased to have some of the best
pilots in the business.

BEN. Unfortunately, none of them are on this flight.

SHELLEY *puts on a velvet eye-mask.*

LINDA. Are you listening to the fella, Shell?

SHELLEY. What's the point? If it goes down, we're doomed.

BILL. We'd like to take a few moments to tell you about the
important safety features of this aircraft.

BEN. There may be fifty ways to leave your lover but there's
only four exits from this aircraft. Please take a moment to
locate the nearest one.

JAN. How long are we stopping in Dubai?

PEARL. Four hours.

JAN. I don't know what we'll do for all that time.

PEARL. Shop.

JAN. I've heard they buy and sell their wives out there. Don't
you go wandering off.

PEARL. Do you think they'd give us owt for Shelley?

JAN. We'd have to pay them.

BILL. Please ensure your seat belts are secured low and tight about your waist. To fasten the belt, insert the metal tab into the buckle and pull –

BEN. Though if you don't know how to operate a seat belt by now, you probably shouldn't be leaving the country unsupervised.

LINDA. Not nervous are you, Shell?

SHELLEY. No. I just don't like the take-off and landing.

LINDA. That's the best bit.

SHELLEY *lifts her eye-mask.*

SHELLEY. Hang on? When have you been abroad?

LINDA. Every November with me nan. Her friend had a flat in Alicante.

SHELLEY. November?

LINDA. She didn't like the heat.

SHELLEY. It's Spain. What else do you go for?

LINDA. All-day breakfasts. Bingo.

SHELLEY. The *vida loca*, eh?

LINDA. Yeah. It were lovely.

SHELLEY *flips the eye-mask down dismissively.*

BILL. In the event of a sudden loss of cabin pressure, oxygen masks will descend from the ceiling. Stop screaming, grab the mask, and pull it over your nose and mouth, like so.

BEN. If you are sitting next to a small child or someone who is behaving like a small child, put on your mask first.

BILL. If you are traveling with two small children, please take a moment now to decide which one you love the most.

JAN. Pearl? I think the Imodium just might have kicked in.

PEARL. Good.

JAN. But if there is any movement, you'll be the first to know.

BEN. In the seat pocket in front of you is a card illustrating the safety features of this plane and the all-important brace position. In the event of cabin pressure rising, it may prove useful as a fan.

BILL. Passengers will be pleased to learn we can land on water. Unfortunately, we can't take off again, so please note your life-jackets are located under the seats.

BEN. Cushions can also be used for flotation aids so in the event of an emergency water-landing, please take them with our compliments.

PEARL. Amazing, in't it? Flying. I mean, how do they ever get a plane off the ground? What kind of mind worked that out?

JAN. It's best not to dwell.

BILL. In a moment, we'll be turning off the cabin lights. This is for your comfort and to enhance the appearance of your flight attendants.

BEN. If you're afraid of the dark, reach up and press the yellow button. This turns on your reading light.

BILL. Please don't press the orange button unless you absolutely have to. This is your ejector seat.

The engines rev up.

JAN. What's that?!

SHELLEY. Frigging hell!

PEARL. You know, we take all this for granted.

BEN. When the seat belt sign is switched off, move about as you wish but please stay inside the aircraft until landing.

JAN. Pearl?!

SHELLEY. Lin?

SHELLEY *grabs* LINDA*'s hand.*

PEARL. We forget what a miracle it is.

JAN. Miracle?

BILL. Finally, as you exit the plane, please make sure to gather all of your belongings. Anything left behind will be distributed evenly among the cabin crew.

LINDA *lifts up* SHELLEY*'s eye-mask.*

LINDA. You're all right, Shell.

BEN. Once again, thank you for choosing to go hurtling through the sky in a metal tube with British Airways. It's our pleasure and privilege to take you for a ride.

SHELLEY *and* JAN. Oh my God.

LINDA *and* PEARL. We're off!

BILL *and* BEN. Enjoy your flight.

The engines roar. The aeroplane takes to the skies.

Scene Four

Thirty-seven hours later. Sydney Airport. PEARL, JAN *and* LINDA *wait with luggage on a trolley.*

TANNOY (*voice-over, Australian accent*). Please help us to keep security alerts to a minimum by keeping your luggage with you at all times.

LINDA. How long has it took again?

PEARL. Ten hours to Dubai; four-hour stop. Eight to Singapore; four-hour stop. Eight from Singapore to Sydney. Three hours sat here.

LINDA. And it's still yesterday at home.

PEARL. I feel like Doctor Who.

LINDA. I feel like one of his monsters.

PEARL. You all right, Jan?

JAN. I don't know what I am.

Beat.

LINDA. He's probably stuck in traffic. He'll be here in a minute.

PEARL. Course he will.

Beat.

LINDA. He'll be here.

Enter SHELLEY.

LINDA. Any luck, Shell?

SHELLEY. According to the bloke, they're in soddin' Singapore.

PEARL. They'll turn up.

SHELLEY. Four Burberry cases? They'll have 'em open on a market stall by now.

LINDA. You've not brought owt valuable, have you?

SHELLEY. No, Linda. Only Prada and Gucci and Jimmy Choo shoes. And my iPod and my BlackBerry and my spare bloody mobile –

LINDA. Well, there you are then.

SHELLEY. I've lost thousands of pounds worth of designer clobber. I've got one pair of pants and I'm in 'em.

LINDA. This happened to my nan once in Alicante. After that, we went prepared.

LINDA *opens her handbag and takes out a pair of pants.*

PEARL. You'll have 'em back in a day or so, they'll send 'em on to the hotel.

LINDA. I packed another toothbrush and a spare pair of smalls.

SHELLEY *holds up the large pair of pants.*

SHELLEY. Smalls?

PEARL. Beggars can't be choosers.

SHELLEY. I'd rather go commando.

SHELLEY *throws the pants back at* LINDA.

PEARL. She was trying to help.

SHELLEY. If we'd flown first class, this would never have happened.

PEARL. So you've said.

LINDA. We wouldn't have got here no quicker.

SHELLEY. We'd have had leg room. We'd have slept.

LINDA. I slept.

SHELLEY. And hogged the armrest all the way. If we'd have flown first class –

PEARL. It would have cost more than the holiday, leave it.

SHELLEY. So? We've got the money.

PEARL. Not for long, the way you're carrying on.

SHELLEY. Well, there's no point hanging around waiting. Let's go to the hotel.

PEARL. We will in a bit.

SHELLEY. Where's Joe got to? Is he fetching us a taxi?

LINDA. He's not here.

PEARL. Not yet.

SHELLEY. But I've been queuing for hours. Where is he?

PEARL. On his way.

SHELLEY. We landed weeks ago. Have you rung his mobile?

PEARL. He's not got one, apparently. He didn't want the stress.

SHELLEY. Well, has he left a message?

PEARL. No.

SHELLEY. He's gone AWOL in the outback?

PEARL. No.

SHELLEY. It happens all the time. I saw *Wolf Creek*. People go out there and disappear.

JAN. He's not disappeared. Not like that, anyway.

TANNOY (*voice-over*). Please be advised that smoking is not permitted in the terminal building, except in designated areas.

SHELLEY. So deport me.

SHELLEY goes to light a cigarette.

PEARL. Oh, no you don't.

PEARL takes her cigarette.

LINDA. You can't mess about here, the coppers carry guns.

SHELLEY. Let 'em shoot me. What do I care? I couldn't feel no worse.

LINDA. My legs have gone to jelly.

PEARL. It's jet-lag, that's all. Yes, we're tired and we're hungry, but at least we've arrived. The holiday starts here, eh?

Beat.

JAN. He's dumped me.

SHELLEY. I knew it. I knew he'd let you down in the end, they always do.

PEARL. Thank you, Mystic Meg.

SHELLEY. I'm telling you, Jan, you're better off without him. The trouble with men is –

JAN. Can we go please?

LINDA. Where to? He's booked the hotel. He's planned everything for us.

PEARL. He has. So let's give him half an hour at least.

JAN. I need a bed. I need to sleep. I need to get out of here.

PEARL. All right, all right. Let's find somewhere by the airport for the night? There might be a message in the morning.

SHELLEY. And if there's not, we're going here.

LINDA. Where?

SHELLEY *takes a magazine cutting from her bag.*

SHELLEY. I saw it in *Heat*. It's got the lot: sun, sea, sand.

LINDA (*reads*). 'The Palazzo Versace.' (*She pronounces it to rhyme with 'face'.*)

SHELLEY (*correcting her*). Versace.

PEARL. What's that when it's at home?

SHELLEY. It's on *I'm a Celebrity*.

LINDA. In the jungle?

SHELLEY. Surfers Paradise. The Gold Coast. It's where they stay before and after.

PEARL. What's it like?

SHELLEY. Only the most glamorous hotel in Oz.

PEARL (*reads*). 'To extend her signature label into a landmark hotel, Donatello Versace brings together inspiration and influences from around the globe.'

SHELLEY. It's got king-sized beds with spa baths. Thirty puddings on the buffet, look. Beauty rooms, bathrobes.

PEARL. We'd be fish out of water.

SHELLEY. Why? Our money's as good as anyone's.

PEARL. But I bet it costs the earth.

SHELLEY. Course it does, but we're living the dream. And don't we deserve a bit of pampering after this?

PEARL. I suppose we do, yeah.

LINDA. I don't mind paying. I'll treat us.

PEARL. No, you won't.

LINDA. But I want to.

PEARL. Forget it.

SHELLEY. Pearl, if she's insistent –

PEARL. She's not. We're going Dutch, we agreed.

SHELLEY. Are we going to Surfers, that's what I want to know?

PEARL. What do you think, Jan? Do you want to head on up there?

JAN. I want to go home.

Beat.

PEARL. Girls? Why don't you get us a cab?

SHELLEY. Forget him, Jan. He's left you high and dry, so what? It's time to move on.

LINDA. Already?

SHELLEY. I *am* a celebrity. Get me out of here! Linda?

Exit SHELLEY *and* LINDA, *pushing the trolley.*

PEARL. Jan, there'll be an explanation.

JAN. There is. I'm dumped.

PEARL. But he phoned you at the weekend –

JAN. That was then. Shelley's right. When I got divorced, I vowed I'd never –

PEARL. Do you want to stay in Sydney? He might turn up, you never know.

JAN. I do.

PEARL. Well, let's at least leave a message at the desk?

JAN. Saying what? 'Came halfway across the world. Sorry we missed you.' He's gone, Pearl. And he's made a bloody fool of me.

PEARL. He has if you let it wreck the trip. You've got four whole weeks of freedom: money in your pocket, time on your hands and no one to please but yourself. When was the last time you had that, eh?

JAN. I can't do it. I can't do four weeks out here feeling like this.

PEARL. You won't. I'll make sure of it. Come on, you can't let me down.

JAN. What do you mean, let you down? It's not my fault he's –

Enter LINDA.

LINDA. Pearl, you'd better come quick. Shelley's flagged down a limo. She's loading all the bags in –

JAN. All he had to do was turn up.

PEARL. It's still the trip of a lifetime without him, luv.

JAN. Yeah. My lifetime. I should have known.

Exit JAN.

LINDA. What now?

PEARL. Try the Gold Coast, I reckon. It'll be no fun stopping in Sydney after this.

LINDA. But what if he's just late?

PEARL. He's had a year to get here.

Beat.

Let's go.

Exit LINDA *and* PEARL.

Scene Five

A week later. Surfers Paradise, Queensland. Morning.
SHANE, *a surfer, is waxing his board.*

SHANE. Fresh board wax – the most beautiful smell in the world. It's all you need on a day like today: the sun on your back, the sand at your feet and the waves out there waiting. Call me a beach bum if it makes you feel better, but I know what I am. I know who I am. Me and my mates, we've come down since we were kids. We've broken boards and bones, and not just our own. When the tourists come to steal the waves, we let 'em know the score. Drop in on us and you'll regret it, mate. That's how it goes down here: to get respect you gotta give it. And the ocean gets the most respect of all.

Enter CHARLIE, *an ageing English hippy aristocrat, carrying bongos. He settles down in his usual spot and lights a huge spliff.*

CHARLIE. Ocean child.

SHANE. Charlie.

CHARLIE. Are we 'ripping the barrels'?

SHANE. Mate, you gotta see! We're making ten-foot waves out there, we're flying.

CHARLIE. Aren't we all?

CHARLIE *plays the bongos, heightening the drama of* SHANE'*s story.*

SHANE. Yesterday, I see my mate shredding one from the back and it's just like a movie, only better. Then a double overhead-plus set appears on the horizon. It's coming for us and coming fast. I thought 'This is it, Shane. This time you've bought it for sure.' We're out there scratching for our lives. We're making the waves by the skin of our teeth but then the rips go against us, we lose our boards and we're down in the water with the stingers and the sharks. A plunging wave pulls us under but somehow we push through. We're home and dry. Lying in the sand and laughing like hyenas, and back to do it all again today.

CHARLIE. Beautiful.

SHANE. I know. Surfers Paradise, for sure.

Enter PEARL, JAN, SHELLEY *and* LINDA, *wearing beachfront de rigueur.* JAN *and* LINDA *wear full-length towel ponchos.* PEARL *wears a hat with corks.* SHELLEY *has designer beachwear.*

They are singing the Home and Away *theme tune.*

CHARLIE. It was once upon a time.

CHARLIE *and* SHANE *watch and listen to the girls, occasionally exchanging a look and a shake of the head between them.*

SHELLEY. Have I died and gone to heaven?

PEARL. Stunning, in't it?

LINDA. Was the sea ever that blue at home?

PEARL. Not in Patrington Haven.

CHARLIE *punctuates the conversation with his bongos.* SHELLEY *gives him a disapproving look.*

SHELLEY. Shall we walk on a bit?

JAN. I've got to stop. I'm sweating cobs.

SHELLEY. Lose the poncho.

JAN. When there's a dirty great hole in the ozone up there?

LINDA. I like 'em.

SHELLEY. You would.

JAN. And everybody's wearing 'em.

SHELLEY. Not at the Palazzo Versace.

PEARL. Palazzo Nowt, there's a McDonald's next door.

LINDA. Jan?

LINDA *takes a photograph of* JAN *in her poncho.*

SHELLEY. It don't matter. We're amongst the *fashionista.*

JAN. What? Old men in white trousers with young leggy blondes.

PEARL. Sugar daddies.

JAN. Sugar grandaddies.

SHELLEY. Millionaire playboys, you ought to get in.

JAN. I might not have a choice if we stay there much longer. Five hundred dollars a night and for what? A funny-shaped bath and a chocolate on your bed.

SHELLEY. That's typical of Jan. She knows the price of everything and the value of nowt.

PEARL. You've got to admit, Shell, it is a bit steep.

SHELLEY. We're living *la moda*.

PEARL. And how come you're suddenly Italian?

SHELLEY. *Scusi?*

JAN. What's with the Cornetto ad?

SHELLEY. I can't help it. I keep gerrin' took for Donatello.

PEARL. More like doner kebab. It's no better than Blackpool here.

SHELLEY. I think it's very cosmopolitan.

PEARL. What bit of it, exactly? Sea World, Wet 'n' Wild or Warner Brothers Theme Park.

LINDA. I liked Sea World.

PEARL. I know you did, but you can hardly call it culture.

LINDA. I liked the fish and the frogs.

PEARL. But you could be out there scuba-diving, seeing 'em for real?

LINDA *approaches* CHARLIE *with her camera.*

LINDA. Excuse me? Would you mind taking us a picture?

CHARLIE. Delighted.

PEARL. You're English?

CHARLIE. I was. I think I'm over it now.

CHARLIE *takes the camera, and the girls gather into a group.*

PEARL. Come on, girls. Big smiles.

CHARLIE. Ready?

CHARLIE *unsteadily puts the plastic camera on the ground.*

SHANE. Not again.

CHARLIE *is about to stamp on the camera when* SHANE *whips it out from under his foot.*

SHELLEY. Oi?

PEARL. What do you think you're doing?

JAN. That's criminal damage.

CHARLIE. A photograph steals the soul. And this place has been pillaged.

SHELLEY. He's off his head.

CHARLIE. Unlike yourselves, who remain trapped in yours.

CHARLIE *offers* PEARL *the spliff.*

PEARL. You're all right.

CHARLIE. Indeed I am. But the question is, are you?

SHANE. Come on, Charlie. Chill out.

SHANE *draws* CHARLIE *away.*

SHELLEY (*looking at* SHANE). Aye-aye.

PEARL. Is he always like this?

SHANE. He's been here a long time, he's seen a lot of changes.

JAN. Well, it's no good blaming us. We're spending hundreds of pounds here, what does he contribute?

SHANE. A bit of colour.

JAN. Colour didn't build those big hotels. It's people like us who make this place what it is.

CHARLIE. Quite.

SHELLEY. He's a nutter.

CHARLIE. Indeed I am. Thank you so much. Goodnight.

CHARLIE *returns to his bongos, punctuating the girls' conversation at intervals.*

LINDA. My camera.

SHELLEY. Not so fast. (*To* SHANE.) *Buona sera.*

SHANE. G'day.

SHELLEY. Would you mind?

SHELLEY *gestures to the camera.*

SHANE. Sure. All together, girls?

SHELLEY. Me first.

SHELLEY *poses on her own.*

PEARL. Look at this. *Baywatch* returns.

JAN. More like *The Monster from the Deep.*

LINDA. That's how she is when we go to the clubs. I tell her, 'Shell, just be you,' but does she listen?

SHANE *takes the picture.*

SHELLEY. *Grazie*, er . . .

SHANE. Shane.

SHELLEY. Oh, what a coincidence. I'm Shelley.

SHANE. Is it?

SHELLEY. So where are you taking me?

SHANE. Huh?

SHELLEY. You can show me the sights if you like?

PEARL. Here we go.

SHANE. I'm kinda busy.

SHELLEY. Doing what?

SHANE. Riding the waves.

JAN. Well, that's his excuse.

SHELLEY. Oh? Well, is there room for little me on the back?

SHANE. Sorry, sweetheart. Surfing's not a tourist ride. It's a religion.

SHELLEY. You're not God-squad, are you?

SHANE. It's a screwed-up planet, right? But out there, it disappears. You've got somewhere you belong, something to believe in.

PEARL. Go on.

SHANE. And you're learning from the ocean every day. For every perfect turn you dig a rail, but that's what it's all about. That feeling of communion.

SHELLEY. Of what?

SHANE. But one day, I'll get a twenty-footer. I'll catch it just right; drop down like I'm falling into hell; pull right, make a swooping turn and go like an express train to the shore. Thirty seconds of heaven and a high to last for ever.

LINDA. Wow!

SHELLEY. Whatever.

PEARL. That's what I've come for, an' all.

SHELLEY. Surfing?

PEARL. No. Salvation.

SHELLEY. She's had a whiff of that spliff.

SHANE. You won't find it here, lady.

PEARL. Well, I know that much. What do you suggest?

Beat.

SHANE. Go west. Go as far as you can, then go some more.

PEARL. I will.

Beat.

SHANE. I hope you find it.

PEARL. I'm glad you have. You're lucky to live in the place you belong.

SHANE. Don't I know it? Surf's up. Oo-roo.

Exit SHANE.

SHELLEY. How can someone so fit be such a freak?

JAN. Never mind him. Can we decide what we're doing for dinner?

LINDA. I'd be happy with a sandwich.

SHELLEY. That's the story of your life.

PEARL. And then we plan our next move, eh?

LINDA *has her Gold Coast brochure.*

LINDA. We could do this. (*Reads.*) 'Whales in Paradise. Don't just whale-watch. Be there! See the magnificent humpback whale breach. Hear the great tail slap the water. Marvel at their playfulness. Feel the waves rock your boat.'

JAN. I don't know about rocking. Is there nowt more sedate?

LINDA (*reads*). 'King Tut's Putt Putt. Come and experience the awesome adventure of Ancient Egypt and the ferocious Jurassic dinosaurs. Fully themed eighteen-hole mini golf course.'

JAN. Is there owt with them little animals?

LINDA (*reads*). 'Lamborghini Experience.'

JAN. That's them.

LINDA. 'Cruise through the streets of Surfers Paradise in a 600 horse-power V12 million-dollar monster.'

SHELLEY. It's a car.

JAN. Is it?

LINDA. You were thinking of wallabies. There's them here an' all, look –

PEARL. Girls, I think it's time for Uluru.

LINDA. Where's that again?

PEARL. The Red Centre. Right in the middle of the country. We'll get a tour bus out there, see all there is to see.

SHELLEY. Like what? Miles and miles of road.

JAN. And burning hot sun.

PEARL. We'll go tomorrow.

JAN. Now hang on –

PEARL. Jan, this place won't heal your heartbreak. We've done the posh hotel bit, now it's time to go bush.

SHELLEY. If you think I'm camping out with the snakes –

PEARL. You don't mind 'em at Versace.

JAN. How long will it take to get there?

PEARL. On the bus? A couple of weeks.

SHELLEY. Weeks?

PEARL. Stopping off every night. They do organised tours. You swap your suitcase for a backpack and you go.

JAN. Two weeks on a bus . . .

SHELLEY. To the back of beyond.

JAN. Four women on our own, is that wise?

LINDA. We're not on our own. We've got each other.

PEARL. Thank you, Linda.

SHELLEY. And you're not getting me out there, no way.

JAN. I'm not sure, Pearl. There's things to consider.

PEARL. Like what?

JAN. My bowels, for one. Does the bus have a ladies?

PEARL. Can we at least discuss this over dinner? The trip I mean, not *that*.

LINDA. Well, I'm hungry.

SHELLEY. Prawns by the pool?

JAN. I could probably choke down something.

PEARL. Right. Good. Back to the hotel, then?

CHARLIE whacks the bongos.

JAN. For a bit of peace and quiet.

SHELLEY. Leave the beach to the bums.

Exit SHELLEY and JAN.

LINDA (*to* CHARLIE). I weren't stealing nothing. I just wanted you to know.

Exit LINDA.

PEARL. She weren't.

CHARLIE. My dear, we're thieves from our very first breath. We take what we can to survive.

CHARLIE takes a spliff from an oversized cigarette case.

PEARL. And that's what you take, is it?

CHARLIE. So they tell me.

PEARL. You know, the sixties never swung as far as Hull. Or the seventies, come to that. Well, not for me. I was busy being a wife and bringing up the kids. But do you think you can turn back the clock?

CHARLIE. Turn and twist it, I've found.

PEARL. With that?

PEARL gestures to the spliff he's about to light.

CHARLIE. It's the road to nowhere, my dear. But at least it's the scenic route.

PEARL. How much?

CHARLIE. The more, the better.

PEARL. I mean how much will you sell us one for?

Beat.

CHARLIE. My dear, I'm no dealer.

PEARL. Can't you make an exception?

CHARLIE. Why?

PEARL. Because I've never had the chance. Because I've only ever had an ordinary life.

CHARLIE. An ordinary life . . .

PEARL. Because they say you should try everything once, while you still can.

Beat.

CHARLIE. I came here in 1968. On the way from somewhere to something, who knows? I had a private education, a trust fund, a future. I was desperate to be ordinary. It all went up in smoke.

CHARLIE *gives the spliff to* PEARL.

PEARL. What do I owe you?

CHARLIE. Nothing. Nothing at all.

Exit CHARLIE. PEARL *looks at the spliff. Enter* JAN.

JAN. Pearl, are you all right?

PEARL *hides the spliff.*

PEARL. Fine.

JAN. I turned round and you were gone. I thought, 'Oh my God, what's happened now?'

PEARL. I'm just having a moment.

JAN. Can't you have it in the shade?

PEARL. I was thinking how we're lucky it's worked out like this.

JAN. What?

PEARL. Joe not showing up. The next two weeks. The outback trip.

JAN. But we haven't agreed to –

PEARL. No map, no plan, no one showing us the way. For the first time in our lives, we're on our own.

JAN. Hang on? You said it was an organised tour.

PEARL. I'm talking metaphorically. Spiritually.

JAN. And I'm talking toilets. I'm still not back to normal and –

PEARL. I really want to do this, Jan. I need to do it.

Beat.

JAN. Why?

PEARL. I can't tell you. Not yet. But when I've worked it all out in my head . . .

JAN. Just a minute . . . you're not all right, are you?

PEARL. I will be.

JAN. You're not. And I've been so full of Joe and . . . Pearl, what's going on?

PEARL. We're off to Uluru, that's what. First bus out. Please?

Enter LINDA.

LINDA. Pearl? Shelley's stopped off at the cocktail bar. She's asking 'em for Sex on the Beach.

Beat.

JAN. First bus out.

Exit PEARL, JAN *and* LINDA.

Scene Six

Two weeks later. Evening. Edge of an outback town. Derelict shack.

DANNY, *a traveller, is watching as his billy – a metal can with a wire handle, suspended over the fire – boils.*

DANNY. Billy tea. An old bushy custom. We've all got our own way of doing it. First, you boil your water. Throw in a fistful of tea and add one for the pot. Leave it on the fire till the tea starts to bubble round the edge. Add your gum-tree leaves to make it settle. Then put your hat in your hand, pick the billy up and swing.

DANNY *picks up the billy with his hat and swings it over his shoulder, down to his knees and over his head, three times.*

Three of these sink the leaves to the bottom of the pot. Take your brew mug and pour. Beauty.

Enter JOE, *carrying a backpack and swigging a can of beer.*

JOE. Excuse me, mate? Where's the campsite?

DANNY. What campsite?

DANNY *pours himself a cup of tea.*

JOE. I went to find a hostel in town but there in't one. Someone said there was a campsite.

DANNY. This is it, mate.

JOE. Where? There's nowt here.

DANNY. There's the land and the stars. What more do you want?

JOE *looks around.*

JOE. I didn't mean to come this far. I think I took the wrong turn.

DANNY. For sure. You're way off the tourist track.

JOE. I have been since I got here.

DANNY. Pommie?

JOE. How do you guess?

DANNY. Here. Get this down you.

DANNY *gives* JOE *a cup of billy tea.*

JOE. I've got my beer, ta.

DANNY. Dehydrates you, mate. Sit down and sober up. You can hit the hay here tonight.

JOE. You mean it?

DANNY. I said it, didn't I? And I don't rate your chances out there on your own.

JOE. Ah, thanks, mate. Thanks a million.

DANNY takes the bread off the fire and gives it to JOE.

DANNY. You'd better help me out with this, too.

JOE. What is it?

DANNY. Damper bread. Dip it in your tea, mate. A taste of Australia.

JOE. Australia. I've had my fill of that.

DANNY. How come?

JOE. It's a long story.

DANNY. I've got all night.

Beat.

JOE. Three weeks ago my girlfriend Jan flew out here with her mates. Dream holiday. They'd had a stroke of luck, you see? Their six-horse accumulator won at Royal Ascot. They got half a million quid between 'em.

DANNY. Strewth.

JOE. And they thought they'd blow a stack of it out here with me. But when they flew in, I was stuck in the Blue Mountains.

DANNY. Bushfires?

JOE. Worst they've had in years. All the power was out, all the phone lines were down. By the time I got to Sydney, they were long gone. I flipped. Took a plane, then a train, then a bus. I had to get away from it. Get lost.

Beat.

DANNY. And now what?

JOE. I've got a week left out here, that's all I can tell you.

DANNY. So you're staying pissed till then?

JOE. What else can I do?

JOE *takes a swig of lager. Silence falls.*

DANNY. You been to Uluru?

JOE. No. I was waiting. I was gonna take Jan. Surprise her, you know?

DANNY. I'm heading up there on the bike. It's eight hundred Ks. Open up the throttle, we could do it in a day.

JOE. We?

DANNY. I can't leave you out here on your own.

JOE. But you've only just met me? You don't even know my name.

DANNY *offers his hand.*

DANNY. Danny.

JOE. Joe.

DANNY. I trust my instincts. Good to know you.

JOE. You an' all, mate. You don't know how good. All these months I've been here and you're the first bloke I've met who's –

DANNY. They were tourists. I'm a traveller. And there's room on my bike for two. You coming?

Scene Seven

Next day. Campsite, Uluru. Late at night.

PEARL, JAN, SHELLEY *and* LINDA *are sitting around a barbecue, drinking beer. Their* GIRLS ON TOUR *T-shirts are now filthy, ragged and wringing with sweat.* LINDA *is serving sausages.*

LINDA. More snags?

JAN. You've picked up the lingo, Lin.

SHELLEY. I've picked up the lice.

PEARL. But we've made it. We're arrived.

SHELLEY. How the hell did we ever let you talk us into this?

LINDA. It's not been as bad as all that, Shell.

JAN. It's been good.

PEARL. Think of all the things we've seen.

LINDA. Kangeroos and emus and wombats in the wild.

JAN. The Great Ocean Road.

PEARL. MacKenzie Falls and Hollow Mountain. The views across the Grampians, I'll never forget it.

SHELLEY. The underground bunkhouse at Coober bloody Pedy, that were five-star luxury, weren't it?

LINDA. The Murray River.

JAN. The sheep station.

PEARL. The Parachilna Gorge.

SHELLEY. My face in the mirror this morning, Jesus wept.

PEARL. And now here we are.

LINDA. Uluru. Snag?

PEARL. Ta.

SHELLEY. Why can't we stay at the resort? It's only down the road. There's shops and bars and a five-star hotel.

LINDA. I like camping.

SHELLEY. You would.

PEARL. And it's the outback we've come for.

JAN. To commune with nature.

SHELLEY. To look at a rock.

JAN. It's quite something, I'll grant you.

PEARL. It's just a shame we can't climb it.

LINDA. Why can't we? Snag?

SHELLEY. No.

PEARL. When you do, you cross a dream track or summat. It's a sacred site. The Aborigines don't stop you but they'd rather you didn't.

LINDA. Best not, then. Snag?

JAN. Snag.

SHELLEY. I don't know why. Charge a tenner a time, they'd make a fortune.

PEARL. We can walk around the base, though. Watch the sun rise, they say it's spectacular.

JAN. We'd better have an early night if we're getting up for that.

SHELLEY. Getting up? I'm not going to bed. Well, I say bed, I mean a hole in the ground.

PEARL. Shelley, it's all part of the experience.

SHELLEY. What? Sleeping in a body bag?

LINDA. A swag.

JAN. Al fresco, under the stars.

SHELLEY. With all them wotsits waiting to pounce.

LINDA. What wotsits?

SHELLEY. Them with the beady eyes.

LINDA. Werewolves?

PEARL. Dingos.

JAN. There's only one dingo here and it's in Prada.

PEARL. It's a brave 'un that'd take a bite of you, believe me.

SHELLEY. The whole country's crawling. I swear to you, if I find a spider in my swag –

PEARL. You won't.

SHELLEY. If one so much as touches my leg, I'm straight to that hotel up the road.

LINDA. It'd probably be scareder of you, Shell.

SHELLEY. I'm not scared. I just think they're shifty nasty creepy –

PEARL. What's your problem, Shelley?

SHELLEY. One: it's too hot. Two: I'm covered in dust. Three: the mozzies think I'm lunch. Four: it's miles to the bog.

PEARL. Go in the bushes.

SHELLEY. Five: my hair's collapsed. Six: it's dark.

LINDA. There's a full moon.

SHELLEY. Exactly. Seven: if owt with more than four legs comes near me, I've got to kill it.

PEARL. Kill it? How can you sit here and still talk like that? After all we've seen out there, how can you think we've got the right?

SHELLEY. It's nature an' all, in't it? Survival of the fittest.

PEARL. Fit for what? Look what we're doing with our fossil fuels and Starbucks.

SHELLEY. There's nowt wrong with Starbucks. They could do with one out here.

JAN *finds a packet of Tim Tam biscuits.*

JAN. Tim Tam?

LINDA. Ta.

PEARL. You've not seen none of it, have you, eh? You've done the whole tour with your eyes shut.

SHELLEY. I like civilisation, what's wrong with that? I like traffic and street lights and bars with nice settees.

PEARL. Where you sit on your silly arse and moan your life away.

SHELLEY. Excuse me? What's bitten you?

JAN. We're just a little bit tired and emotional, that's all.

PEARL. You won't do this, you don't want that, you can't
    possibly go there –

JAN. Look, it's been a long trip but we're here now. All we've
    got to do is sit back and relax.

SHELLEY. In the dirt.

PEARL. See? She never stops.

SHELLEY. What's wrong with wanting a bed and a bath?

LINDA. Shall we have a sing-song?

PEARL. It's more than that, and you know it.

LINDA (*singing*).
    'Waltzing Matilda,
    Waltzing Matilda,
    You'll come a-waltzing Matilda with me.'

LINDA *and* JAN (*singing*).
    'And he sang as he watched
    And waited till his billy boiled.
    You'll come a-waltzing Matilda with me.'

    Silence.

LINDA. What's the next bit?

JAN. I don't know, Linda.

LINDA. Is there one?

JAN. It's like 'God Save the Queen'. There's more verses to
    that an' all, we learned 'em at school. There's the bit you
    always sing and then it's:

    (*Singing.*)
    'Oh Lord our God arise – '

PEARL. I wouldn't. Not here.

JAN. Why not? She's their Queen an' all. They're still a
    Commonwealth nation.

LINDA. What's that?

JAN. Ruled by us.

PEARL. Years ago.

JAN. It were the days of the Empire, Lin. Great Britain owned a third of the globe.

SHELLEY. How come we stopped sending convicts, that's what I'd like to know? I'd love to see them bad lads from our estate put out here.

LINDA. They'd graffiti the rock.

SHELLEY. Three times I've been burgled since the win, and have they done 'em? The coppers even know who it is.

JAN. When Claire's car was broken into, she didn't even report it. 'What's the point?' she says.

SHELLEY. She's right. They've gone feral. They should lock 'em up and throw away the key.

JAN. Still . . . it all seems like a long, long way away.

Beat.

LINDA. What time is it back home?

JAN. Ten to four yesterday.

LINDA. Blimey.

JAN. Claire'll be in lectures.

LINDA. The girls'll be at work.

SHELLEY. Them robbing gets'll be going through my drawers.

JAN. It's all going on without us. This must be what it's like when you die.

SHELLEY. That's it, cheer us up.

JAN. I think about it sometimes, don't you?

LINDA. A bit.

SHELLEY. I'm starting to wish for it.

JAN. I lie in bed and wonder what it's like to not exist?

PEARL.
'Ay, but to die and go we know not where;
To lie in cold obstruction and to rot.'

JAN. You what?

PEARL.
'This sensible warm motion to become
A kneaded clod; and the delighted spirit
To bathe in fiery floods or to reside
In thrilling region of thick-ribbed ice.'

LINDA. Who said that?

PEARL. Shakespeare.
'To be imprisoned in the viewless winds
And blown with restless violence round about
The pendent world.

SHELLEY. Go on, get the party started.

PEARL.
' 'Tis too horrible.
The weariest and most loathed worldly life
That age, ache, penury and imprisonment
Can lay on nature is a paradise
To what we fear of death.'

LINDA. How come you know it off by heart?

PEARL. We did it at school. *Measure for Measure*. I went to
the library and dug it out last year. Mick thinks I'm mad but
I love it. I recite it when he's out.

LINDA. Do you know any more?

SHELLEY. Please, no.

PEARL.
'Love is not love
Which alters when it alteration finds – '

SHELLEY. For God's sake, Pearl. Get a life!

PEARL. And what does that mean exactly? 'Get a life'?

SHELLEY. Cheer up and have a bit of fun.

PEARL. And is that what we're here for? Is that what living is? You can't 'get' a life – you *are* a life.

SHELLEY. Whatever.

PEARL. And what does that mean? 'Whatever'?

JAN *recites the first line of the novel,* Rebecca *by Daphne du Maurier.*

LINDA *recites the first two lines of 'Like a Prayer' by Madonna.*

JAN. That's lovely, Linda. Where's it from?

LINDA. 'Like a Prayer'. Madonna.

JAN. Oh.

LINDA *recites the next two lines.*

PEARL. Home . . .

JAN. I know.

PEARL. All them things you fill your day with. You really think they matter. You really believe they're who you are.

JAN. When I go back, things are changing. I'm changing, I can feel it.

LINDA. How?

JAN. Joe didn't show but I survived. No, I've done more than survived it. I'm feeling things I've never felt before. I think I'm feeling strong.

LINDA. When I go home, I'm doing good. I'm going to properly help folk. Neighbours an' that.

SHELLEY. You've been watching too much soap.

LINDA. Why should I have all this when they've got nowt?

SHELLEY. All what?

LINDA. The money. I can help 'em.

JAN. Linda?

SHELLEY. You can't go giving it away.

LINDA. Yes, I can. It's easy. I've done it before.

SHELLEY. Who to?

LINDA. A girl I went to school with. Kelly.

SHELLEY. Never heard of her.

LINDA. She came round the other week. She's got three kids
and no fella. She's having it hard, so I said I'd help her out.

JAN. She came asking?

LINDA. Not as such. But I think perhaps she'd heard about the
win.

SHELLEY. I think perhaps she had, yeah.

JAN. And how much did you give her?

LINDA. Not as such.

JAN. How much?

LINDA. Just enough to clear her debts. She was dead nice
about it, dead appreciative, you know?

SHELLEY. How much?

LINDA. Fifteen hundred, that's all.

JAN. How much?!

LINDA. I told her it were best if she kept it to herself but
I think she might have let on. People from the pub, they've
been knocking at the door. 'I can't pay my council tax. My
boiler's broke down. I need money for the meter.' I've been
saying no, but it's not right.

SHELLEY. They're not right.

LINDA. Some woman came knocking the night before we left.
Said her grandson were poorly. She just wants him to go
swimming with dolphins.

JAN. That costs thousands.

LINDA. Five thousand. And I can't get it off my mind. I should
have helped her. I've got all this and she's got nowt.

SHELLEY. She's got a bloody good scam on the go, you mean.

JAN. If you can't handle your money, you can get an adviser.

LINDA. It's not hard to handle. It's just hard to have. 'Cos it makes you think 'Why me?' It makes you feel guilty.

SHELLEY. But you don't help a loser by being one yourself.

LINDA. They're not losers, they're just struggling. We all know what that's like.

SHELLEY. They're spongers, they're piss-takers –

LINDA. I don't care. If they want the money, let 'em have it. I just want things to go back to how they was.

PEARL. You're not the only one.

SHELLEY. Linda, you don't have to give them to chavs on the estate. You can let me help you. I can show you how to shop.

PEARL. One for her, two for you, eh? Bloody hell, Shelley, you're supposed to be her friend.

SHELLEY. And you're supposed to be mine, but you've done nowt but bloody get at me all week.

JAN. Tim Tam?

SHELLEY. What's the matter, eh? What have I done?

PEARL. You really want to know? I find you selfish and shallow –

LINDA. Pearl?!

PEARL. And totally incapable of . . .

PEARL*'s voice breaks*.

JAN. Pearl?

LINDA. What's up?

SHELLEY *gathers up her stuff*.

SHELLEY. Well, they say you don't know someone till you go away with them.

LINDA. Where are you going?

SHELLEY. To that hotel.

JAN. It's miles away.

LINDA. It's dark.

SHELLEY. I don't care.

JAN. There's dingos.

SHELLEY. Let 'em start, I'm ready.

Beat.

PEARL. Shelley, I'm sorry.

SHELLEY. Too late.

PEARL. I didn't mean to have a go, it's just . . .

JAN. What?

PEARL. It's just –

Enter DANNY.

DANNY. Excuse me, ladies? I'm looking for my mate. English fella. So high. Baseball cap.

JAN. I'm sorry, luv, we've not seen him.

SHELLEY. We've not seen no one till now.

DANNY. We pitched up. He went off. Call of nature. He'd had a couple of beers, I think he's lost his way back.

PEARL. It's easily done out here.

DANNY. I'll say. You've pitched up right on the edge of things.

PEARL. That's how we like it.

JAN. Peace and quiet.

SHELLEY. That's how some of us like it.

DANNY. I hear you. Sorry to have troubled you, ladies.

DANNY *turns to go.*

SHELLEY. So if we see him, shall we tell him you were looking?

DANNY. Sure.

SHELLEY. And your name is?

DANNY. Danny.

SHELLEY. Danny? What a coincidence. I'm Shelley.

Enter JOE, *singing 'Danny Boy'.*

DANNY. Talk of the devil. Mate, where've you been?

JAN *sees* JOE.

JAN. That's what I'd like to know.

SHELLEY. Oh my God!

PEARL. Joe?

JOE. Jan?

DANNY. *The* Jan?

JOE. I can explain –

LINDA. What's going on?

JAN. You tell me.

PEARL. We're not in Kansas any more, are we?

SHELLEY. Dead right.

DANNY. Welcome to Oz.

End of Act One.

ACT TWO

Scene One

Music – traditional Aboriginal.

Later that night. Campsite, Uluru. DANNY *and* LINDA *are sitting together, watching the horizon.* PEARL *and* SHELLEY *are sitting apart.* SHELLEY *is smoking; both are listening to* DANNY *and* LINDA.

DANNY. They say when the sun rises, the rock glows orange. The lighter the sky, the brighter the rock. Then in a single moment, there's birdsong, the sun comes up and it's on fire.

LINDA. I can't wait.

DANNY. The Anangu see this as the heartbeat of the world. The centre point. Creation, religion, culture, life and death: it starts and ends here.

LINDA. How?

DANNY. They say there's a hollow underneath the rock. It holds an energy source; that energy created their ancestors and they made the world from the Dreamtime.

LINDA. The Dreamtime . . .

DANNY. Where past, present and future come together all at once.

LINDA. So everything that's happened – and is going to happen – is happening now?

DANNY. Yeah.

LINDA. Quiet for such a busy place, in't it?

DANNY. That's the myth, anyway. Except it's not a myth to the Anangu. They've only got the one word for knowledge and belief, there's no difference to them. They look inside the rock. They listen. They understand.

LINDA. Did you grow up with it all?

DANNY. Me? No, I'm a Bankstown boy.

LINDA. What's that?

DANNY. Bankstown. Western Sydney. About as far from here as you can get. Drugs. Gangs. The whites against the Lebs, a lot of aggro. But I'm not a fighter. I bought a bike and hit the road.

LINDA. Have you not got a job?

DANNY. I've been a farmhand and a shearer. I've been out at Coober Pedy mining opal.

LINDA. We went there, didn't we, Shell?

DANNY. I work, I travel. I live on the road.

LINDA. You couldn't do that at home, you'd end up dead in a ditch.

DANNY. All you want out here is the land and the sky.

LINDA. Not a house? Not someone to come home to?

DANNY. The Anangu say the more you know, the less you need.

Beat.

LINDA. I've got a terrapin. Tony. We pack fish all day, you see? It's nice to come home and see summat swim.

DANNY. Guess it is.

LINDA. And then there's Patrick, he's my pen pal. I met him at the races. He rides horses all over, so I don't see him much. He sends me postcards though. Says he's thinking of me.

DANNY. Beauty.

LINDA. Who thinks about you? Your family?

DANNY. I'm a bushwhacker. I left all that behind.

LINDA. Not if you believe in the Dreamtime.

DANNY. I don't know what I believe in. But perhaps we'll see it in the sunrise, eh?

DANNY *contemplates the horizon.*

LINDA. Danny?

DANNY. Yeah?

LINDA. I know it's not very spiritual, but I need the loo.

DANNY. No worries.

LINDA. You know, with you being a bush bloke? Will you come with me? Stand guard while I . . .

DANNY *stands up and holds out his arm.*

DANNY. Linda, I'd be honoured.

LINDA *takes his arm. Exit* DANNY *and* LINDA.

PEARL. Who do you think he is, then?

SHELLEY. Joe's mate.

Beat.

PEARL. He's latched on to Linda.

SHELLEY. People do.

Beat.

PEARL. Nice lad, in't he? Nice-looking?

SHELLEY. Shall we cut the chit-chat, eh? It's shallow.

PEARL. Shell –

SHELLEY. You're all right, I am. And I don't care neither. All the deep people I've met are miserable.

Beat.

PEARL. It's being out here together, that's all. 24/7. It's hard. It takes its toll.

SHELLEY. You're telling me.

PEARL. It's not you, Shelley. I just want things to be perfect, that's the problem.

SHELLEY. But it's not. It never will be. I'm me and you're
you. We're chalk and cheese, we always was. At work, it
didn't matter 'cos we had the routine, but here . . .

PEARL. You've hated every minute of it, haven't you?

Beat.

SHELLEY. No. I just feel like I've left myself somewhere,
that's all.

Beat.

PEARL. You're right. We should have stayed at the resort.

SHELLEY. Well, maybe Jan'll thank you?

PEARL. Should we go and find her? See if she's all right?

SHELLEY. She'll be back when she's done.

PEARL. What are the odds, eh? Meeting up like this?

SHELLEY. Bigger than the jackpot.

PEARL. So perhaps we've come here for a reason after all?

SHELLEY. Or one of them spirits is playing silly buggers.
Either way, feels like the joke's on us.

Beat.

PEARL. Just when you think you've got it all worked out, just
when things are going your way, it's always then.

SHELLEY. What is?

PEARL. Luck changes. Life is what happens when you're
making other plans. Whoever said that were spot on.

SHELLEY. I don't do plans no more. They never work.

PEARL. But how else do you live?

SHELLEY. Day to day. Hour to hour.

PEARL. And you look for distractions.

SHELLEY. You do, yeah.

PEARL. Distractions like this.

PEARL *gets the spliff out her bag and gives it to*
SHELLEY.

SHELLEY. Pearl?!

PEARL. It's a bit battered, but I think it's all right.

SHELLEY. Where did you get it?

PEARL. That bloke on the beach.

SHELLEY. How long have you been into this?

PEARL. I'm not. I've never done it before. But now we're
here . . .

SHELLEY. Me and you?

PEARL. I can't do it on my own, I don't know how.

SHELLEY. It's not rocket science.

PEARL. But it'll send me somewhere, won't it? If I try it just
the once?

Beat.

SHELLEY. What's going on with you, Pearl? What's it about?

PEARL. I will tell you, Shell. Just not now, eh?

SHELLEY. Not till you've . . .

SHELLEY *offers* PEARL *the spliff.*

PEARL. I think you better light it.

SHELLEY. Yeah?

PEARL. Before they all get back.

SHELLEY. Are you sure about this?

PEARL. You're not getting cold feet on me, are you?

SHELLEY. Me? No way!

SHELLEY *lights the spliff and inhales.*

PEARL. Is it all right, then?

SHELLEY. It will be in a minute.

SHELLEY *offers it to* PEARL.

PEARL. Bloody hell, Shell. What am I doing?

SHELLEY. Getting a life. Well?

PEARL *takes the spliff.*

PEARL. Whatever.

Scene Two

Same time. Campsite, Uluru. JAN *and* JOE *are deep in conversation.*

JOE. You must have seen 'em on the news? They burned for ten days straight. I were trapped, all the bloody roads were closed.

JAN. Couldn't you have gone another way?

JOE. Five hundred miles they spread. That's London to Glasgow. Did you not see the smoke?

JAN. We didn't stay in Sydney. We went up the coast.

JOE. Well, I tell yer, I've never seen owt like it. Flames two hundred feet high and all these volunteer blokes going out to fight 'em.

JAN. You don't get that in the travel brochures, do you?

JOE. It were devastated, Jan. And so was I.

JAN. Really?

JOE. What do you think? I was going off my head. I was coming in two days early, sorting the hotel, getting everything straight. I had it planned.

JAN. Me an' all.

JOE. And when I did get to the aiport, there's no message, no nothing. I got through to Mick but he said you'd hit the road. What did you do that for, eh? How come you never left word?

JAN. I thought you'd dumped me.

JOE. After everything I said on the phone?

JAN. I thought you'd changed your mind.

JOE. Why would I?

JAN. Loads of reasons. All sorts of things.

JOE. What?

Beat.

JAN. I just thought you had, that's all.

JOE. Jan, you coming out here, it's what kept me going.

JAN. What do you mean? You've had the time of your life.

JOE. Oh aye, I've done it all, me. Sydney Opera House, Byron Bay, Fraser Island. And they're full of clicky gap-year kids with backpacks for brains; and beautiful views of the bottom of a glass; and hostels full of strangers who snore in seven languages.

JAN. But you said it was fantastic?

JOE. Course I did. I thought if you believed me, I might start to an' all.

Beat.

JAN. How come you never told me?

Beat.

JOE. I couldn't. This was it, my great escape. I weren't meant to be out here missing home. Missing you.

JOE *goes to touch* JAN *but she moves away.*

JAN. I've been up all night. It's hot. I need a bath.

JOE. And I don't?

JAN. I mean it, Joe. I don't feel . . .

JOE. What's up?

JAN. Well, it's a lot to take in, don't you think?

JOE. I know, it's unbelievable, finding you like this.

JAN. When you didn't turn up, I thought you'd dumped me. I thought you'd gone off with some Aussie girl.

JOE. Me?

JAN. Maybe I wanted to think it. Joe, I'm not sure I want it.

JOE. Want what?

JAN. You. All this. I've been on my own a long time –

JOE. So have I, a bloody year.

JAN. Things have changed. I've changed. I'm just not sure any more.

Beat.

JOE. So how come you've come out?

JAN. Well, it was booked.

JOE. You could have cancelled.

JAN. How could I? The girls were so excited, you know what they're like –

JOE. You came here for them?

JAN. Not just for them. For me an' all. To prove something to myself, I think.

JOE. Prove what?

JAN. I don't know, Joe. I turn up here and you're gone, then suddenly we meet up in the middle of nowhere. It's not real –

JOE. 'Tis for me. It's fate.

JAN. It's not what life's about. Not for people like us. All right, we had the win, but that were a one-off. We don't just walk off into the sunset –

JOE. We don't have to. We can go to that hotel down the road.

JAN. Why?

JOE. I don't want to marry you, Jan. I just want to be with you, that's all.

JAN. What? Now?

JOE. I fancy you rotten, I have done for years. At home you said to wait, but for what?

JAN. The right time.

JOE. Five in the morning. Uluru. It's the right time for me.

JAN. We can't. The girls.

JOE. I'll have you back before they know it.

JAN. Joe –

JOE. Come on, why not?

JAN. 'Cos I don't do things like that.

JOE. But you can if you want to. And I think you do. Deep down.

JAN. Here? Right now? Us?

JOE. No time like the present. Seize the day. And if you don't want me tomorrow . . .

Beat.

JAN. This is not what I do.

JOE. Nor me. Are we going or what?

Scene Three

Later. Uluru. PEARL *and* SHELLEY *are stoned.*

PEARL. What's it called again?

SHELLEY. What?

PEARL. That thing we're here for?

SHELLEY. Yuraloo?

PEARL (*laughing*). What sort of name is that?

SHELLEY (*singing*).
'But dreaming's yuraloo
Why aren't they coming true?'

PEARL *and* SHELLEY *sing the verse of 'I Should Be So Lucky' by Kylie Minogue.*

SHELLEY. Snogs?

PEARL. Oh yeah, I'm starving.

SHELLEY. Snogs.

SHELLEY *raids the frying pan for sausages.*

PEARL. When does it start, then?

SHELLEY. What?

PEARL. The way it's meant to make you feel, when does it kick in?

SHELLEY. It has.

PEARL. Give 'em here, then.

PEARL *stuffs a sausage into her mouth. Enter* LINDA *and* DANNY.

SHELLEY. Linda!

LINDA. What?

SHELLEY *hugs* LINDA.

SHELLEY. You're so lovely, aren't you? Underneath.

LINDA. What's up with you?

SHELLEY. Snog?

LINDA. No.

LINDA *pulls away from her.*

PEARL. You all right, Linda?

LINDA. Fine, yeah.

PEARL. So are we. We're having the crime of our life.

LINDA. You've made it up?

PEARL. Course we have.

SHELLEY. We're the best of mates for ever.

LINDA. Good. So you're going to watch the sunrise with us?

PEARL. All the way to the toppermost of the poppermost.

SHELLEY. Oi? (*To* DANNY.) Crocodile Dundee? Snog?

DANNY. No, ta.

> SHELLEY *offers* DANNY *the spliff.*

SHELLEY. I bet you'll have some of this, though?

PEARL (*laughing*). Shell?!

DANNY. No.

SHELLEY. Oh, go on, 'mate'. It's dead ripper and bonza, in't
   it, Pearl?

PEARL. It's 'pearl'. That's what Aussies call a thing they like,
   I've heard 'em. Pearl.

SHELLEY. Lin?

> SHELLEY *offers* LINDA *the spliff.*

LINDA. That's what them kids on our stairwell are smoking.

SHELLEY. Nah. It's not like you get at home, this.

LINDA. My mum used to do it an' all with her mates. I know
   the smell.

PEARL. These snogs are fantastic.

LINDA. Where did you get it? Where?

DANNY. Linda, leave 'em to it, eh?

LINDA. No. I've seen what it does.

SHELLEY. Linda, with respect, you know bog all about it.

LINDA. I do, as it happens. There's a crack house at the end
   of our road.

SHELLEY *and* PEARL *burst out laughing.*

It's not funny!

DANNY. Come on, let 'em sober up.

LINDA. Pearl, you don't even smoke.

PEARL. I used to years ago. I drank Babycham an' all, by the bucket.

LINDA. If your Mick could see you now; and your kids and your grandson. What would you say to him, eh?

PEARL. That life is for living. And at my age it's the things you've not done you regret.

SHELLEY *sings 'Que Sera Sera' by Doris Day,* PEARL *joining in.*

DANNY. Linda, the sunrise.

LINDA. It's the money again.

SHELLEY. It's nowt to do with that, she got it free.

LINDA. It's changed you. It's changed us all.

SHELLEY. Linda, will you come down off your horse-high?

PEARL. Your what?

LINDA. We should have never won it, it's brought us nowt but trouble.

PEARL. Shell, I wanna tell you summat.

SHELLEY. What?

PEARL. What I said to you. I'm truly, madly, deeply sorry.

SHELLEY. Forget it.

PEARL. I mean it. And you're not like chalk or cheese, you're a mate.

SHELLEY. So are you.

PEARL. A proper mate.

LINDA. It's ruined everything.

PEARL *continues to sing 'Que Sera Sera'.*

Where is it? Where's the stash?

SHELLEY. Stash? Who are you, The Sweeney?

PEARL. Charlie's Angels?

SHELLEY. Juliet Bravo.

PEARL. I loved that.

LINDA *grabs* PEARL*'s bag.*

LINDA. It's wrong. It's not what we came here for.

PEARL. Now then, Lin . . .

LINDA *searches through the bag.*

LINDA. It's going on the fire.

DONNY. Linda –

PEARL. That's private . . .

LINDA. I don't care. It's wrong. It's . . .

LINDA *takes a leaflet from the bag.*

PEARL. What?

LINDA. What's this?

Beat.

PEARL. Nowt.

LINDA *looks at the leaflet.*

LINDA. Who gave you this?

SHELLEY. What?

LINDA *passes the leaflet to* SHELLEY.

LINDA. Pearl, you don't know someone who's . . .

PEARL. I do, yeah.

SHELLEY. Who?

Beat.

PEARL. Me.

*The sun rises over Uluru: a burst of birdsong and vivid,
glorious orange.*

Scene Four

Dawn. Campsite, Uluru. DANNY, SHELLEY, LINDA *are
listening to* PEARL, *the sunrise forgotten.*

PEARL. They called me for a mammogram. Had it done,
usual thing, thought nowt more about it. A week or so later,
there's a letter from the hospital, a thick 'un with a map,
I thought 'Eh-up?' They wanted me in, but said I weren't to
worry 'cos most things they look at are benign. They did a
needle biopsy, an ultrasound scan. I went back the next day
for the results. They didn't say what type it is and I didn't
ask. I've got it and they're treating it, that's all I need to
know. When I go back in, they take the lump, not the breast.
Well, I say lump, I still can't feel it. They take lymph nodes
an' all, just to see if they're involved. You're in a couple of
nights then you're home.

LINDA. When? When do they do it?

PEARL. The week we get back.

DANNY. You came all this way knowing that?

PEARL. What else was I to do? Sit at home whittling?

LINDA. What does Mick say about it?

PEARL. Not much. He doesn't know.

LINDA. You've not told him?

PEARL. I couldn't. Not before I went away. And when I talk
to the family, I'll have to deal with them. Till then, I'm
dealing with me.

LINDA. How do you mean?

PEARL. When I opened that letter, summat happened in my

head. It was like I stepped outside myself. All day at the hospital, I watched myself go through it. And I watched all them couples sat there rigid with fright. I thought, 'Pearl, you can't go there. You've got to fight the cancer not the fear.' I know I can. I just had to come out here to be sure.

DANNY. So when they've took it away, what then?

PEARL. Radiotherapy to kill off what's left.

SHELLEY. Will you lose your hair?

PEARL. That's chemo. It won't come to that. I'm not gonna let it.

Beat.

LINDA. You'll be all right, Pearl.

PEARL. Course I will.

SHELLEY. You'll be fine.

PEARL. I won't *be* fine, I *am* fine. I feel on top of the world. They've caught it and they'll sort it. I've been lucky.

Beat.

LINDA. I don't think we should stay out here no more.

SHELLEY. Nor do I.

LINDA. We should fly back to Sydney. Get our cases sent out, find a nice hotel, see the sights.

PEARL. Fine by me. I think we could do with a bit of five-star fun. Shell?

SHELLEY. Fine.

PEARL. But I don't want tears or special treatment. It's the last week of the holiday. Let's make it the best, eh?

LINDA. We will.

SHELLEY. Yeah.

DANNY. And as I won't be there, can I do this?

DANNY *gives* PEARL *a big hug.*

PEARL. You can do it as much as you like, luv.

DANNY. You're pearl, Pearl.

PEARL. Ta.

DANNY. Go for your life, eh?

PEARL. Just watch me.

Enter JAN, *scrubbed clean and shining.*

JAN. Morning!

PEARL. Is it? I've lost track.

JAN. How was the sunrise? I missed it. I was otherwise
engaged.

PEARL. Have you sorted things out?

JAN. Oh, yes.

PEARL. Where is he, then? Where's Joe?

JAN. In the hotel bar. Danny? Joe said to tell you the beers are
on him.

DANNY. Right.

PEARL. Have you had one an' all?

JAN. Why? Do I look different?

LINDA. You've been for a shower.

JAN. I have. And I can't tell you how good it was.

PEARL. Jan –

JAN (*to* DANNY). Please don't think me rude, but I just want
a word with the girls. A private word.

DANNY. No worries. I'll be off.

PEARL. You're all right, Danny. I tell you what, Jan. Let's go
for a walk. I need to stretch my legs a bit, come on.

JAN. A walk?

PEARL. Yeah. The sun's up, and I've got a bit of news.

JAN. My God, so have I.

PEARL. Well, don't keep me in suspense then. You first.

Exit JAN *and* PEARL.

LINDA. I can't believe it. Pearl? It's not right, it's not fair –

SHELLEY. Why don't you go with 'em?

LINDA. I don't know what to say. I don't know what to do –

SHELLEY. Just go!

LINDA. Shell?

SHELLEY. Please.

LINDA *looks at* DANNY, *who nods in encouragement.*

DANNY. Go.

Exit LINDA, *after* PEARL *and* JAN.

SHELLEY (*to* DANNY). You an' all.

SHELLEY *starts to pack up the camp.*

DANNY. What are you doing?

SHELLEY. You heard 'em. We're leaving.

DANNY. Just sit down here a minute –

SHELLEY. Are you deaf? I said go.

Beat.

DANNY. No worries.

DANNY *nods and goes to leave. When he looks back, he sees* SHELLEY *fighting tears.*

SHELLEY. Christ . . .

DANNY *unties the scarf around his neck and offers it to her.*

DANNY. Shelley? I don't have a handkerchief but this does the job.

SHELLEY. I'm not crying.

DANNY. Well, have it just in case. Go on.

SHELLEY *takes the scarf.*

SHELLEY. It just brought summat up, that's all. It brought summat back . . .

DANNY. Tell me. You might as well. You won't see me again.

Beat.

SHELLEY. My mum was hit by a car. When they told me, it was just like that. Normality then – wham.

DANNY. She came through it but – ?

SHELLEY. No. There was only me and her, so they put me in care. Got fostered. Nice people, but I never fitted in. Your friends become your family – or as close as you can get.

DANNY. It's ten years since I last saw mine. Big heap of shit it was, at home. If I hadn't shot through, I'd have ended up just like 'em. Still, you think of 'em sometimes.

SHELLEY *offers the scarf back.*

SHELLEY. Ta.

DANNY. Keep it.

SHELLEY. For what? I don't do tears. Like Pearl says, they don't help.

SHELLEY *returns to clearing up.* DANNY *looks to the outback.*

DANNY. You know, you could always go out there and let it out? I did. Rode out as far as I could and then some. Rode till no one could see me but the spirits. Screamed and cried, man. Set it free.

Beat.

SHELLEY. I don't know what you mean.

DANNY. Everyone else does. What makes you different?

SHELLEY. Hang on. You don't know me, you know nothing about me. I'm not like this in real life, I don't even look like this. I lost my suitcases in Singapore and . . .

SHELLEY *is close to tears again.*

DANNY. It's all right.

SHELLEY. It's not. I'm meant to be a model. I'm all set to launch.

DANNY. Right.

SHELLEY. And I will when I get home. I will, so that's it. Subject closed.

Beat.

DANNY. I hope you make it, Shelley.

SHELLEY. Course I will. I've been told I've got the look.

DANNY. I don't mean the modelling.

Beat.

SHELLEY. If you don't mind, I really do want to be on my own.

Beat.

DANNY. I hear ya.

SHELLEY. See you, then.

SHELLEY *returns to packing up.*

DANNY. It's been good to know you, Shelley.

SHELLEY. You don't.

DANNY. It's been good.

DANNY *tips his hat and turns to go.*

SHELLEY (*screams*). Frigging hell!!

DANNY. What?

SHELLEY. A spider, it bit me.

DANNY. Where?

SHELLEY. On my hand.

DANNY. I mean where is it?

SHELLEY. Over there somewhere! Kill it, quick!

DANNY. Show me.

>   DANNY *looks at* SHELLEY*'s hand.*

SHELLEY. Just there, look.

DANNY. Where?

SHELLEY. There. I bet it's venomous, an' all.

DANNY. I can't see any bite.

SHELLEY. I felt it. Find it, quick! Go on! Kill it before it
strikes again.

>   SHELLEY *bursts into tears.*

DANNY. Hey? You don't do tears.

SHELLEY. I do for friggin' spiders. Help me, please?

>   *Beat.*

DANNY. All right, little fella. Where are you hiding?

SHELLEY. It ran that way.

DANNY. This way?

SHELLEY. Yeah. I think so. I don't know.

>   DANNY *hunts for the spider.*

DANNY. Come out with your hands up. All eight of 'em,
come on.

SHELLEY. This one had more than eight, I swear.

DANNY. Little devils, aren't they?

SHELLEY. They're horrible. If I find one in the flat, I'm a
wreck.

DANNY. Well, don't you worry. This one's bought it for sure.

SHELLEY. I got one in the home once, it had legs as long as
mine. It was one of them what's too big to kill. You could
see its black eyes, like it's coming to get you.

DANNY. Gotcha!

DANNY *grabs the spider and cups it in his hand*.

SHELLEY. Oh my God!

DANNY. There he is.

SHELLEY. Well, get rid of it! Tread on it, then.

DANNY. No need. This one's one of the good guys. He didn't bite you. He's a wuss, aren't you, fella?

DANNY *approaches* SHELLEY *with the spider*.

SHELLEY. Frigging Ada!

DANNY. Look. Toothless.

SHELLEY. Don't you bring it near me!

DANNY. He won't hurt you.

SHELLEY. Don't you dare!

DANNY. He just wants to say g'day.

SHELLEY. Well, I bloody don't.

DANNY *offers* SHELLEY *the spider*.

DANNY. You might be glad you did.

SHELLEY. No way.

DANNY. He's harmless.

SHELLEY. No! No, no, no, no, no!!

Beat.

DANNY. What's going on? You're not scared of a little thing like this?

SHELLEY. It's not little.

DANNY. Go on. Take him.

SHELLEY. No.

DANNY. I'm here, you're all right.

SHELLEY. No!

DANNY. For me. No, for you.

SHELLEY. What do you mean?

DANNY. You don't want to live like this.

SHELLEY. It's not my fault, I can't help it. I can't help the way I am.

DANNY. You can. You can take him. Take him.

DANNY *extends his cupped hands.*

SHELLEY. I can't.

DANNY. Give me your hand.

SHELLEY. I mean it, I can't.

DANNY. You can. Come on, your hand.

SHELLEY. And then what?

DANNY. You take him and you let him go. It's easy.

SHELLEY. Easy to say.

DANNY. It's mind over matter. Are you ready?

SHELLEY. No.

DANNY. Why not?

SHELLEY. 'Cos I'm scared, aren't I?

DANNY. Of what? It's nothing. Trust me. Take him.

Slowly, SHELLEY *extends her hands to take the spider.*

SHELLEY. Oh . . . my . . . God!

DANNY *goes to release the spider into her hands.*

DANNY. See?

SHELLEY *has her eyes closed.*

SHELLEY. Do it, then.

DANNY. I have.

SHELLEY. But I can't . . .

SHELLEY *opens her eyes and looks into her hands.*

There's nowt there.

DANNY. Exactly.

SHELLEY. Where's it gone? What have you done?

Beat.

DANNY. Think about it.

Beat.

SHELLEY. I didn't make it up. There was a spider, I felt it.

DANNY. Sure there was. But all the rest came from you.
Change your thoughts, you change the world.

DANNY *turns to go.*

SHELLEY. Danny? How do I change this?

DANNY. What?

SHELLEY. I won some money a while back. A hundred grand.
Left my job. Went shopping. New kitchen, new bathroom.
Got my teeth done and my tits. Now I've got shoes I'll
never wear and bags I don't want. I've got a Cartier watch
but I can't work the cooker. I drink and smoke and go
clubbing on a Monday. I mean, how sad is that? All the men
I meet are arseholes and I miss my mates at work. I'm
twenty-six years old, so I've missed the modelling boat. I
think I've missed the boat, full stop. I'm stuck in Hull and
I've got three grand left. Three grand to pay for all this,
then I'm back in the fish plant.

DANNY. Shelley –

SHELLEY. It's all right. I don't want your sympathy. I just
wanted to . . . Well, like you said, I'll not see you again. I
just wanted to say it out loud.

DANNY. I'm glad you did.

SHELLEY. Good. So off you go, then. Have a drink with Joe.

DANNY. I don't have to –

SHELLEY. Yes, you do. I've got to sort all this out, go on.

SHELLEY *gathers up all their belongings.*

DANNY. Do your mates know you're going back?

SHELLEY. I'll tell 'em when I'm ready. And I know what
you're thinking. She's selfish and shallow and you're right,
I am. But you've not seen where I come from, it's not
lovely like this. I just want to live the dream a bit longer,
that's all.

DANNY *takes* SHELLEY's *hand and kisses it.*

DANNY. Go for your life.

Exit DANNY.

Scene Five

A few days later. Sydney, a street. Enter KOALA BARE, *a
glamorous drag queen, with a pink bucket to collect money.*

KOALA. Welcome, welcome, welcome to the 2007 Sydney
Gay and Lesbian Mardi Gras! For the twenty-ninth year
we're here to liberate and celebrate our gay, lesbian,
transgender, bisexual and queer brothers and sisters all
across our great nation. You've never been to a party till
you've seen Mardi Gras. It's a fair, a festival, a parade; a
civil rights march for equality, acceptance and visibility . . .
and girls, are we visible today!

Enter LINDA. *She looks at* KOALA *in awe.*

Seven thousand beautiful people will be strutting, dancing,
skipping, riding and shimmying down the celebrated
Golden Mile in the name of love, pride and acceptance.
You'll see Dykes on Bikes, Fags with Flags, the Mardi Gras
Marching Boys, Harry Poofters, cheerleaders, exotic
dancers, muscle men and good old-fashioned drag queens;
all together for a night of dazzling satire and outrageous
celebration. So fetch out your best frock, sew on a sequin,
let out your leathers! It's Mardi Gras, people! Give, give,
give!

KOALA *shakes her bucket.*

LINDA. Excuse me?

LINDA *throws some coins into the bucket.*

KOALA. Thank you, gorgeous.

LINDA. Do you always dress like that?

KOALA. Only high-days and holidays. Do you like it?

LINDA. I love it.

KOALA. Well, you can come again.

LINDA. I wish. I've never seen owt like it.

KOALA. Ooh, I love a Mardi Gras virgin.

LINDA. We all are. Me, Pearl, Jan and Shelley.

KOALA. Now there's a bunch of drag queens if ever I heard one.

LINDA. No, they're not –

KOALA. But is it a bunch or a handful? What's the collective noun for drag queens, do you think?

LINDA. We've been in Sydney all week. They'd love to meet you, I bet. I'll bring 'em over if you like?

KOALA. I know! A garland!

LINDA. They're having coffee up the road but I had to come out.

KOALA. You're a dyke?

Beat.

LINDA. I don't think so.

KOALA. Nor me. I dipped in, but khaki's not my colour. What's your name, precious?

LINDA. Linda.

KOALA. *Enchanté*, Linda. I'm Koala Bare. That's B-A-R-E.

LINDA. L-I-N-D-A.

KOALA. So what are you doing in the C-I-T-Y?

LINDA. We're on holiday from England but we go home tomorrow.

KOALA. Well, before you do, here's a little poser for you. Well, quite a big poser in these dainty shoes.

KOALA *strikes a pose.*

Who am I?

LINDA. I don't know.

KOALA. Think! Who do I look uncannily like?

LINDA. No one I know.

KOALA. You do, you do, come on? She's an icon. A superstar. A true-blue showgirl.

LINDA. You're not whatsername, are you? Camilla Parker Bowles? She had a hat with a feather on at Ascot.

KOALA. She's Aussie.

LINDA. Dame Edna?

KOALA. You're skating on thin ice, Blanche.

LINDA. Give us a clue.

KOALA. I'll give you slap if you don't get it this time. Scott and Charlene? 'The Locomotion'? Two-timing French boyfriend?

LINDA. Kylie?

KOALA. Put the flags out! And for calling me Camilla, you can donate again.

LINDA. What are you collecting for?

KOALA. The lady herself. The Kylie Minogue Breast Cancer Fund.

Beat.

LINDA. Done well, an't she?

KOALA. Well? Is the Pope a closet queen? I saw her comeback show last year. She cried, we cried. She sang 'Over the Rainbow' suspended on a moon, we cried again –

LINDA. Do you take cheques?

LINDA *takes out her cheque book and writes a cheque.*

KOALA. Sure. They reckon there's a couple of hundred Kylies here today but, between you and me, I've got the edge. And the legs, of course. We're both so petite, it's uncanny, I know. If she was here, she'd say, 'Koala, it's like looking in the mirror.'

LINDA *gives the cheque to* KOALA.

LINDA. She would.

KOALA. So what have you given us? Dollars or pounds.

KOALA *looks at the cheque in amazement.*

LINDA. You can convert it, can't you?

KOALA. Hey, big spender . . .

LINDA. I'd better find the girls.

KOALA. What's this?

LINDA. Don't worry, they'll cash it all right.

LINDA *turns to go but* KOALA *pulls her back.*

KOALA. Not so fast, Blanche. Should I know you? Are you some kind of minor royal?

LINDA. No.

KOALA. Ivana Trump's love-child?

LINDA. No.

KOALA. You won the lottery?

LINDA. Sort of.

KOALA. Well, come on, what's the story? You can't run out on me now, this is better than *Hello!*

LINDA. We had a windfall, that's all. I bought a new winter coat and a terrarium and helped out my friend. Well, she weren't my friend really, she picked on me at school but you can't hold that against her. She had trouble at home. And that's more or less what's left.

KOALA. You can't give it all to us?

LINDA. I can. I want to. I've got a personal interest.

Beat.

KOALA. You?

LINDA. No. A friend.

Beat.

KOALA. I'm sorry.

LINDA. Don't be. She's handling it. We had a big talk in Alice Springs, the four of us together. Decided not to bring it up till we got home.

KOALA. And who decided to give us all this?

LINDA. It's a good cause. I'm not.

KOALA. You reckon?

LINDA. Ever since I've had it, I've not felt like me. I don't know what to do with it, I don't know how to be.

KOALA. With a hundred grand? There's only one thing you can be.

LINDA. What?

KOALA. Fabulous.

KOALA *screws up the cheque and throws it away.*

LINDA. But I can't, I'm not, I never have been. I don't like being different. I'm ordinary and plain and –

KOALA. Plain? You're a rainbow. Sun and showers, that's what made you. I can see it in your eyes. You're one of us.

LINDA. As if.

KOALA. Linda, do you think I came out of my mother's womb like this? In little baby platforms, drenched in baby glitter-spray? I was the runt, the class joke, the last to be picked for the team. All I wanted to do was disappear. Tried to vanish at sixteen with a bottle of pills. I didn't want to die but I knew I couldn't live as I was. So I packed my guilt

and shame and brought it to Sydney. Covered 'em in sequins.
Out I came and here I am.

LINDA. What's that got to do with this?

KOALA. Everything. I couldn't change what I was, so I changed
how I felt. I took what didn't fit and made it beautiful,
comprendez?

LINDA. No.

KOALA. Linda, it's not the money you've gotta love. It's you.

Beat.

LINDA. How?

Enter BONDI BITCH, another drag queen.

BONDI. So this is where she's hiding?

KOALA. Hiding? She's been pounding the pavements, which
takes some doing in platforms, let me tell you.

BONDI *looks into the bucket.*

BONDI. Ooh . . . ten minutes' hard labour.

KOALA. That's nine more than you've ever done.

BONDI. I've been working on myself, Blanche.

KOALA. And there's a thankless task.

BONDI. May I remind Mother Teresa we're due on parade?

LINDA. I better leave you to it.

KOALA. Not so fast, Cinders. You're coming with us.

KOALA *drapes her feather boa around LINDA's
shoulders.*

LINDA. Where to?

KOALA. A land far, far away. Behind the moon, beyond the
rain . . .

*Enter PEARL, JAN and SHELLEY, who is wearing
DANNY's scarf.*

PEARL. Here she is.

JAN. Linda, where have you been?

SHELLEY. We thought you'd run away to join the circus.

BONDI. She has. The flea circus.

SHELLEY (*looking at the drag queens*). Friggin' hell. What have you come as?

BONDI. *Touché*, lady, though I use the term loosely.

LINDA. Girls? This is my friend Koala Bare.

KOALA. *Enchanté*.

LINDA. And this one's . . . ?

BONDI. Bondi Bitch.

KOALA. And boy, does she live up to her name.

PEARL. We've got to get a picture of this. Shell, where's your camera?

SHELLEY *gives* PEARL *her camera and the drag queens pose.*

KOALA. So which one are you, dear? Pearl or swine?

PEARL. Pearl.

JAN. And I'm gobsmacked. How do you walk in those shoes?

KOALA. Trade secret.

BONDI. The building trade.

PEARL. Smile then?

BONDI. We don't, dear.

KOALA. Not on camera.

PEARL. All right, say . . .

LINDA. 'Kylie.'

KOALA *and* BONDI *pose.*

KOALA *and* BONDI. Kylie-Queen-of-All-Things-Fabulous.

PEARL *takes a picture*.

PEARL. That's one for the album.

KOALA. Or the police files.

BONDI. And with any luck, I'll be banged up tonight.

PEARL. Are you marching?

BONDI. No, I work in a bank.

JAN. I wish Joe could see all this.

SHELLEY. And Danny.

BONDI. Who's Joe?

PEARL. Her fella.

JAN. No, he's not. He's just a man I know.

SHELLEY. Intimately.

KOALA. Oh?!

PEARL. Don't ask. It's X-rated.

BONDI. We'd love to stop and chat but we've got a carnival to do.

KOALA. And two bishops.

BONDI. Rector?

KOALA. Well, it didn't do her any good.

PEARL. We'll look out for the two of you.

KOALA. The three of us. Linda's coming.

JAN. Our Linda?

SHELLEY. She can't. She's not gay.

BONDI. But nobody's perfect. Are you ready?

KOALA. Your carriage awaits.

LINDA. I can't, not in front of all them people. There's thousands of 'em watching.

KOALA. Hundreds of thousands, but there's safety in numbers.

PEARL. Linda, you've got to.

JAN. You can't miss out on this.

PEARL. It's the chance of a lifetime.

SHELLEY. Can we go, an' all?

LINDA. Oh, can they? Please? We've come all this way
together. It's our last night in Oz.

KOALA. Bondi?

BONDI. They're not friends of Dorothy.

KOALA. But they're friends of Linda, and that's good enough
for me.

BONDI *picks at* SHELLEY*'s outfit.*

BONDI. Well, this one won't look out of place.

KOALA. I'll work on the others. A bit of powder and paint.

LINDA. And we'd never get to do this in 'ull.

BONDI. 'Ull?

LINDA. That's where we're from.

BONDI. 'Ull.

LINDA. It's not as bad as it sounds. It's home.

Beat.

BONDI. 'Ull. You have my deepest sympathy. Koala? Do your
worst.

SHELLEY. Oh my God!

LINDA. Wow!

KOALA. Girls? Quick march.

Exit KOALA, *with* PEARL, JAN, SHELLEY *and* LINDA.

BONDI *turns to the audience and takes the microphone.*

BONDI. Don't look like that or you'll be next. Greetings,
Mardi Gras people. Don't you all look beautiful tonight?

You look particularly lovely, madam. No, really, you do.
I don't care what they say, I love catalogue clothes. And
Miss, your hair's gorgeous. Did you come on a motorbike?
I've been shopping today. I bought some new perfume.
Can you smell my Charlie from there? I bet you can. Now,
I've got a little story for you about three friends of mine:
Cinderella, Tom Thumb and Quasimodo. One day, Cinderella
says to me, 'Bondi Bitch, I must be the prettiest girl in the
world.' Then Tom Thumb pipes up, 'Well, I must be the
smallest.' And Quasimodo says, 'I guess I must be the
ugliest.' Well, let's find out, I said, and I took them to the
place where the prettiest, the smallest and the ugliest are
crowned. They went in one by one. Cinderella came out and
said, 'It's true, I'm the prettiest.' Tom came out and said,
'It's true, I'm the smallest.' Quasimodo came out and said,
'Who the hell is Koala Bare?' Girls and boys and all those
in between: Here she is! Let the carnival begin!

Music: 'I Am What I Am' by Gloria Gaynor.

Enter KOALA, *miming to the first verse of the song.*

Enter PEARL, SHELLEY, JAN *and* LINDA, *marching and
waving, having clearly had a Koala make-over.*

BONDI *takes the second verse.*

KOALA *pulls* LINDA *forward.*

KOALA. Come on, girl!

LINDA. I can't.

KOALA. Yes, you can. Hit it!

LINDA *takes the third verse, out-performing them all.*

Sydney, Australia! I give you Pearl! Jan! Shelley! Linda!
All our sisters!

Exit KOALA *and* BONDI, *marching.* PEARL, LINDA,
SHELLEY *and* JAN *sing, with drag-queen gestures and
outrageous confidence to the song's end.*

Scene Six

Next day. Sydney Airport. Enter PEARL, *juggling suitcase, tickets and hangover.*

TANNOY (*voice-over, Australian accent*). Please be advised that smoking is not permitted in the terminal building, except in designated areas.

Beat.

And nor is that.

PEARL. What?

TANNOY (*voice-over*). Dreading going home. You're ready now. It's time.

Enter JAN, *with baggage.*

PEARL. Did you hear that?

JAN. What?

Beat.

PEARL. This hangover's worse than I thought.

JAN. My head's thumping.

PEARL. How many of them wotsits did we have?

JAN. Daiquiris. I lost count after eight.

PEARL. Good though, weren't it? Being gay for a day.

JAN. Everyone should do it.

PEARL. I'd love to have seen us.

JAN. I still can't believe it. Us, bold as brass, in front of all them crowds.

PEARL. But that's what we came for. Not the carnival, as such. The experience.

JAN. And it's not stopping there.

PEARL. No?

JAN. I'm not going back to the things I had before. *Coronation Street*, takeaways, Saturday nights in. So what if the ironing's not done till tomorrow? From now on, I'm living for today.

PEARL. Me an' all.

JAN. But I'll be there for you, Pearl. Every step of the way.

PEARL. And with a bottle of champagne at the all-clear?

JAN. Bloody oath!

Beat.

PEARL. I'm coming back here with Mick. When all this is done with, I'm bringing him out.

JAN. He won't travel.

PEARL. He will. He'll have to. And once he gets here, he'll love it.

JAN. Have you missed him?

PEARL. I have, yeah. And I never thought I would. I missed them times when you sit there and don't say a word. That feeling of safety, I suppose.

JAN. I missed our Claire, but not as much as I thought.

PEARL. No?

JAN. And you know what's fantastic? I've got things to tell her for the first time in my life. Things I've done, things I've seen, things that happened.

PEARL. Like Joe?

JAN. I might. I'll see. She's a bit narrow-minded.

PEARL. You don't have to give her all the details.

JAN. I can't help it. Once I get on the subject, I can't stop.

PEARL. We've noticed.

JAN. You don't mind, do you? I mean, with all you're going through –

PEARL. Jan, it's the best pick-me-up I could wish for.

Enter SHELLEY, *with a luggage trolley stacked so high with Burberry cases she can't see where she's going. She is still wearing* DANNY's *scarf.*

SHELLEY. Coming through!

JAN. She's got 'em.

PEARL. I knew they'd turn up in the end.

SHELLEY. I never brought all this lot out. I think they've bred 'em.

JAN. Excess baggage? You'll need a private jet.

SHELLEY. I can't even remember what's in 'em.

JAN. Half of Harvey Nicks, I shouldn't wonder.

SHELLEY. Didn't need it, though, did I? Not in the end.

JAN. Are you still on the Daiquiris?

SHELLEY. It just makes you think a bit, that's all.

PEARL. What does?

SHELLEY. All that's happened since we got here. What's happening to you. Last week. Last night. Just makes you think that going back to the fish plant's not the worst thing in the world.

JAN. You?

TANNOY (*voice-over*). Please help us to keep security alerts to a minimum by keeping your memories with you at all times.

Enter LINDA, *with baggage, wearing huge Koala Bare platforms and feather boa.*

LINDA. Are we checking in then?

PEARL. In a minute.

LINDA. I want to go to duty-free. I need some Kylie Darling.

JAN. What's that?

LINDA. Koala gave me a tester. She says I can't leave the country without it.

SHELLEY. It's perfume.

LINDA. Not just perfume. (*Reads*.) 'A gorgeous bright pink fragrance that sparkles like the sequins on a showgirl's costume and makes you want to get up and dance.'

JAN. Very nice.

PEARL. I think we should all have a squirt.

SHELLEY. Dead right. Are we up on the board?

They look up to the departure board. Enter JOE, *carrying his backpack.*

PEARL. Bangkok.

SHELLEY. Adelaide.

JAN. Florida.

LINDA. Peking.

PEARL. Manchester.

JAN. That's us.

JOE. I think that's me, an' all.

The women turn.

PEARL. What are you doing here?

JOE. I booked myself on your flight. Months ago. Surprise.

SHELLEY. In't it just?

LINDA. Perfect timing an' all. We're just checking in. Come on, you can sit with us.

JOE looks at LINDA.

JOE. What happened?

LINDA. Mardi Gras.

JOE. Look, I'm not here to crash your party. I can sit on my own, I'm used to it, I'm fine –

PEARL. No, you won't. He's coming back with us, in't he, Jan?

JOE *looks at* JAN.

JOE. I don't have to, Jan.

JAN *walks over to* JOE *and gives him a big passionate kiss. Claps, cheers and wolf-whistles from the girls.*

Bloody hellfire.

JAN. You'd better believe it.

JOE. Does this mean we're back on?

JAN. Properly on. With proper dates an' that. No more cooking your tea in my kitchen, we're going out. It's on me.

JOE. It's not.

JAN. I'm an independent woman, Joe. Deal with it.

JOE. And I'm your fella. Deal with that.

JOE *picks up* JAN*'s bags.*

PEARL. Right, then. Are we checking in or what?

LINDA. Are we shopping?

SHELLEY. Are we having a sit-down? It's worn me out pushing this.

Enter DANNY.

DANNY. I'm not surprised. The Queen of England travels lighter.

LINDA. Danny!

SHELLEY. What are you doing here?

DANNY. I brought Joe back to Sydney. Thought I'd call on the folks. See a few of the old haunts. It's been a while.

Beat.

Wanna come?

SHELLEY. You what?

DANNY. I'll find a place we can stay. I'll show you the real
  Sydney – how about it?

SHELLEY. All of us?

DANNY. No. Me and you.

  Beat.

SHELLEY. You're asking me to stop on?

DANNY. Sure. And if it works out, we could head down to
  Adelaide? It's a beautiful town. I know a bloke who runs
  a bar, he said there's work there if I want it.

SHELLEY. Works out? Are you having a laugh?

DANNY. No.

SHELLEY. You're having a laugh.

DANNY. Shelley, I'm not the kind of bloke who wears his
  heart on his sleeve, but if I don't say it now, you'll be gone.

SHELLEY. Say what?

DANNY. Stay with me. Stay.

  SHELLEY *just looks at him.*

PEARL. Shell?

JAN. Don't just stand there.

LINDA. Say summat.

SHELLEY. I can't.

  Beat.

  I mean, I can't stay. There's things going off. Things at
  home and I've got to be there.

DANNY. What things?

SHELLEY. You know what.

  SHELLEY *gestures to* PEARL.

PEARL. Shelley –

SHELLEY. And for once in my life, I want to do the right thing. For you and for me.

PEARL. I'll tell you what the right thing is. Turn that bloody trolley round and go with him. I'll see you again before you know it. Me and Mick are coming back.

JAN. And me and Joe.

LINDA. And me. I'm doing Mardi Gras again next year.

SHELLEY. But –

PEARL. But nothing. Life don't throw you many chances, so when it does, you grab 'em.

SHELLEY. But I just want to say . . . Pearl, you've been like a mum to me. And I know I've never told you, but I'm telling you now –

PEARL. And I'm telling you what any mum'd say. Be happy. Go.

SHELLEY *looks at* DANNY.

SHELLEY. Danny, you don't even know me.

DANNY. I trust my instincts. Don't you?

SHELLEY. Well, I never have till now.

DANNY. There's only one problem.

SHELLEY. What?

DANNY *gestures to the luggage*.

DANNY. How do I get that lot on the bike?

SHELLEY *pushes the trolley to* LINDA.

SHELLEY. Linda, you can wear 'em at work. Have summat fabulous under your apron, for me?

LINDA. I will.

JOE *shakes* DANNY*'s hand*.

JOE. Good luck, mate.

DANNY. Likewise.

JOE. And thanks.

Beat.

DANNY. Likewise.

JOE hugs DANNY.

SHELLEY. Now, there'll be none of that for us. No goodbyes, it's not my thing.

JAN. But how else do we go?

LINDA. We say, 'See you tomorrow,' like we used to at work.

SHELLEY. But not yet. I want a picture. Danny?

SHELLEY gives DANNY her camera.

DANNY. All together, girls. Big smiles.

The girls gather together for a picture.

LINDA. Say 'Mardi Gras'.

ALL. Mardi Gras!

DANNY takes a picture.

DANNY. One more.

JAN. 'Uluru.'

ALL. Uluru!

DANNY takes a picture.

DANNY. And one for luck.

PEARL. 'The land of Oz!'

ALL. The land of Oz!!

DANNY takes a picture.

DANNY. Beauty.

PEARL. And as there really is no place like home, we'd better go.

Everyone gathers up their bags.

LINDA. Now?

JAN. Best we do, Lin.

PEARL. So we'll just say –

SHELLEY. See you tomorrow.

PEARL. Bright and early.

JOE. Bright and early? Not this one.

JAN. See you . . .

SHELLEY. Oh, sod this.

 SHELLEY *draws the girls into a hug.*

TANNOY (*voice-over*). Please be advised that crying is not permitted in the terminal building, except in designated areas.

SHELLEY. Go on, then. Bugger off.

PEARL. You bugger off. (*With an Australian accent.*) You go for your life.

SHELLEY. You an' all.

PEARL. Just watch me.

 Beat.

DANNY. Shelley?

 DANNY *puts out his hand.* SHELLEY *gives the girls a last look.*

SHELLEY. I will see you, right?

PEARL. Before you know it.

JAN. Next to no time.

LINDA. Tomorrow.

 Beat.

DANNY. See? The all-at-once time. They're with you.

SHELLEY. You believe that?

DANNY. I know it.

Beat.

SHELLEY. Let's go.

Exit DANNY and SHELLEY, hand in hand.

JOE. Jan?

JAN. I'm here.

Exit JOE and JAN.

LINDA. Pearl?

PEARL. I'm on my way.

Exit LINDA.

PEARL looks after SHELLEY, as if she might follow her.

TANNOY (*voice-over*). Will all passengers for the next part of the journey please proceed to the gate. Pearl? Your luck's not running out just yet. Are you ready?

Through the tannoy, we hear an echo of 'I Am What I Am'.

PEARL. You bet.

PEARL picks up her suitcase and exits.

The End.